FREEDOM'S PROMISE

CH
ON
CY

13/1/2022

D1681121

WE
DEMAND

VOTING
RIGHTS
NOW!

WE
DEMAND

END
BIAS
OW!

NOW!

BY DUCHESS HARRIS, JD, PHD

Core Library

Cover image: The
March on Wash...

...print of Abdo Publishing
abdobooks.com

abdocorelibrary.com

Published by Abdo Publishing, a division of ABDO, PO Box 398166, Minneapolis, Minnesota 55439. Copyright © 2019 by Abdo Consulting Group, Inc. International copyrights reserved in all countries. No part of this book may be reproduced in any form without written permission from the publisher. Core Library™ is a trademark and logo of Abdo Publishing.

Printed in the United States of America, North Mankato, Minnesota
092018
012019

THIS BOOK CONTAINS RECYCLED MATERIALS

Cover Photo: AP Images
Interior Photos: AP Images, 1, 6–7, 12–13, 16, 20–21, 23, 25, 43; Paul Schutzer/The LIFE Picture Collection/Getty Images, 5, 28–29; Bettmann/Getty Images, 9; Red Line Editorial, 19, 37; Francis Miller/The LIFE Picture Collection/Getty Images, 31; akg–images/Newscom, 34–35; Mark Reinstein/Shutterstock Images, 39

Editor: Maddie Spalding
Series Designer: Claire Vanden Branden
Contributor: Martin Gitlin

Library of Congress Control Number: 2018949712

Publisher's Cataloging-in-Publication Data

Names: Harris, Duchess, author.
Title: The march on Washington and its legacy / by Duchess Harris.
Description: Minneapolis, Minnesota : Abdo Publishing, 2019 | Series: Freedom's promise | Includes online resources and index.
Identifiers: ISBN 9781532117725 (lib. bdg.) | ISBN 9781641856065 (pbk) | ISBN 9781532170584 (ebook)
Subjects: LCSH: March on Washington for Jobs and Freedom (1963 : Washington, D.C.)--Juvenile literature. | King, Martin Luther, Jr., 1929-1968. I have a dream--Juvenile literature. | Civil rights movements--Juvenile literature. | United States. Civil Rights Act of 1964--Juvenile literature.
Classification: DDC 323.1196073009--dc23

CONTENTS

A LETTER FROM DUCHESS.................... 4

CHAPTER ONE
He Had a Dream 6

CHAPTER TWO
The Fight for Civil Rights.......... 12

CHAPTER THREE
Planning the March................20

CHAPTER FOUR
Civil Rights Leaders 28

CHAPTER FIVE
A Living Legacy 34

Fast Facts........................... 42

Stop and Think....................... 44

Glossary 45

Online Resources..................... 46

Learn More 46

About the Author 47

Index 48

A LETTER FROM DUCHESS

We are often taught that the best way to understand Dr. Martin Luther King Jr. is through his "I Have a Dream" speech at the March on Washington. While Dr. King dreamed of racial harmony, he also spoke of economic inequality.

People at the march wanted not only civil rights, but also jobs and fair pay. The march was organized by several groups, including the Congress of Racial Equality, the Student Nonviolent Coordinating Committee, the Southern Christian Leadership Conference, the National Association for the Advancement of Colored People, and the National Urban League. Economic justice was a key part of what they were fighting for. Yet people often forget that for King, economic justice was an important goal.

Please join me in learning about the global impact of the March on Washington. Join me in a journey that tells the story of the promise of freedom.

Duchess Harris

A group of protesters gathers near the Lincoln Memorial during the March on Washington.

HE HAD
A DREAM

On August 28, 1963, approximately 250,000 people streamed into Washington, DC. They had arrived in buses, planes, and cars. Some had walked or hitchhiked hundreds of miles to get there. They gathered near the Washington Monument. Then the crowd marched 1 mile (1.6 km) to the Lincoln Memorial. Marchers carried signs that demanded equal rights for African Americans. African Americans wanted to have the same freedoms and rights as white people.

Although most marchers were African American, the crowd included people of

People traveled from all over the country to attend the March on Washington in Washington, DC.

different races and religions. They made a powerful statement. Americans from all backgrounds wanted their country to embrace its values.

Civil rights leaders gave speeches. Among them was Martin Luther King Jr. When it came time for him to speak, the marchers hung on his every word. Millions more people watched his speech on television.

A HISTORY OF HATE

Positive changes had come painfully and slowly in the United

Jim Crow laws separated black people in public spaces, such as waiting rooms.

States. In the 1960s, Jim Crow laws enforced racial segregation in the South. These laws separated black and white people in public places. Black people had to attend separate schools. They had to use separate facilities, such as bathrooms. They had to sit in separate sections on public transportation. These laws were meant to keep black people from interacting with white people. The services and facilities provided for black people were often much worse than those

A REQUEST FROM A FRIEND

The legendary "I Have a Dream" parts of King's 1963 speech were almost never spoken. Toward the end of King's speech, gospel singer Mahalia Jackson shouted to King to "tell 'em about the dream." She had heard King talk about his dream for the future before. King then added what became the most famous part of his speech.

provided for white people. African Americans had also been denied basic freedoms, such as the right to vote. Some people had been killed while fighting for these freedoms.

Such horrors motivated King to talk about his dream for a better future. He spoke about a new nation of togetherness. He envisioned a future in which people would be judged by their character rather than their skin color.

NONVIOLENT PROTEST

King was one of the last speakers at the March on Washington. This march was the largest protest gathering ever held in Washington, DC. It was an important event in the American civil rights movement. This movement had begun nearly a decade earlier. Many civil rights activists had been beaten, arrested, and killed. Some African Americans had become more aggressive in demanding action. But King and other civil rights leaders called for nonviolence. They peacefully protested to create change. Protesters at the March on Washington practiced nonviolence. The televised event captured the nation's attention. It inspired activists to continue to fight for equal rights.

FURTHER EVIDENCE

Chapter One discusses the March on Washington and King's famous speech. What was one of the main points of this chapter? What evidence is included to support this point? Read the article at the website below. Does the information on the website support this point? Does it present new evidence?

KING SPEAKS TO MARCH ON WASHINGTON
abdocorelibrary.com/march-on-washington-and-its-legacy

CHAPTER
TWO

THE FIGHT FOR CIVIL RIGHTS

Laws in the Jim Crow South restricted black people's rights in many ways. Southern states had created laws called the Black Codes in the late 1800s and early 1900s. The Black Codes created obstacles that kept black people from voting. These obstacles included literacy tests, poll taxes, and the grandfather clause. Literacy tests were difficult and confusing. Poll taxes were fines that kept people from voting. The grandfather clause allowed people to vote only if their ancestors had voted. But most African Americans'

Many activists protested segregation laws in the 1960s.

ancestors had not been allowed to vote. So they also were not allowed to vote.

Many white people also used violence to intimidate black people. An all-white organization called the Ku Klux Klan (KKK) was founded in 1866. The KKK hurt and killed black people. Threats of violence kept many African Americans from voting.

Many African Americans moved to northern cities in the early 1900s. They wanted to escape violence in the South. They hoped to find better job opportunities in the North. But racism and discrimination were everywhere. Many employers did not want to hire black people. Some people refused to rent housing to African Americans.

LAUNCHING A MOVEMENT

One black activist who moved from the South to the North was A. Philip Randolph. Randolph moved from Florida to New York City in 1911. He settled in Harlem, a mostly black neighborhood. He quickly became an activist and a leader in the black community. In 1941 he planned a protest march on Washington, DC. The march was meant to protest discrimination in the US military. Black and white soldiers were segregated. They fought in separate units. Black soldiers were often forced into noncombat roles, such as driving trucks.

THE BSCP

In 1925 Randolph founded the Brotherhood of Sleeping Car Porters (BSCP). The BSCP was a labor union. A labor union is a group of workers who organize to demand better working conditions. The BSCP was made up of African American railroad porters. Porters were workers who served passengers on trains. Black porters were often forced to work long hours. They were poorly paid. Through Randolph's leadership, the workers were able to obtain better payment and treatment.

Randolph formed the March on Washington Committee. Committee members helped organize the march. It was planned for July 1, 1941. The organizers expected approximately 100,000 people to attend. President Franklin D. Roosevelt heard about the

A. Philip Randolph was a prominent civil rights leader in the 1960s.

planned march. One week before the march, Roosevelt banned discrimination in military industries. Randolph decided to call off the march. But he continued his civil rights work through the March on Washington Movement (MOWM). The MOWM organized protests for civil rights issues throughout the 1940s.

ACTIVISM AND INTEGRATION

Activists such as Randolph had been protesting against Jim Crow laws throughout the 1900s. But little was achieved until the 1950s. The US military was not desegregated until 1948. School desegregation followed later. In 1954 the US Supreme Court ruled that schools should be integrated. This case was called *Brown v. Board of Education of Topeka*.

Integration came slowly in the South. Black activists tried to integrate public places, such as bus terminals. They staged sit-ins. In a sit-in, protesters would refuse to leave a business that would only serve white people.

In December 1955, Rosa Parks was arrested in Montgomery, Alabama. Parks was an African American woman. She had refused to give up her bus seat to a white person. Activists organized a boycott in response to her arrest. They stopped using buses in Montgomery.

The US Supreme Court ruled against segregation on public transportation in 1960. In 1961 a group of activists called the Freedom Riders tested this ruling. The group was made up of young black and white activists. They rode together on buses in the South. White people, including KKK members, beat up Freedom Riders. On one occasion, they even bombed a bus. The Freedom Riders managed to escape.

The civil rights movement grew in numbers in the 1960s. In 1963 activists organized a series of protests called the Birmingham Campaign. Dr. Martin Luther King Jr. helped launch this campaign. Activists organized sit-ins, boycotts, and marches. The protests

PERSPECTIVES

JOHN LEWIS

African American activist John Lewis was a Freedom Rider. He later became a congressperson who represents the state of Georgia. In 2009 a white man named Elwin Wilson visited Lewis. Wilson had been a member of the KKK in the 1960s. In 1961 he had beaten Lewis at a bus stop in South Carolina. Wilson apologized to Lewis. Lewis was moved by Wilson's apology. Lewis later said: "Elwin Wilson shows us, that people can change. . . . Wilson proves that we are all one people, one family . . . and what affects one of us affect us all."

CIVIL RIGHTS TIMELINE

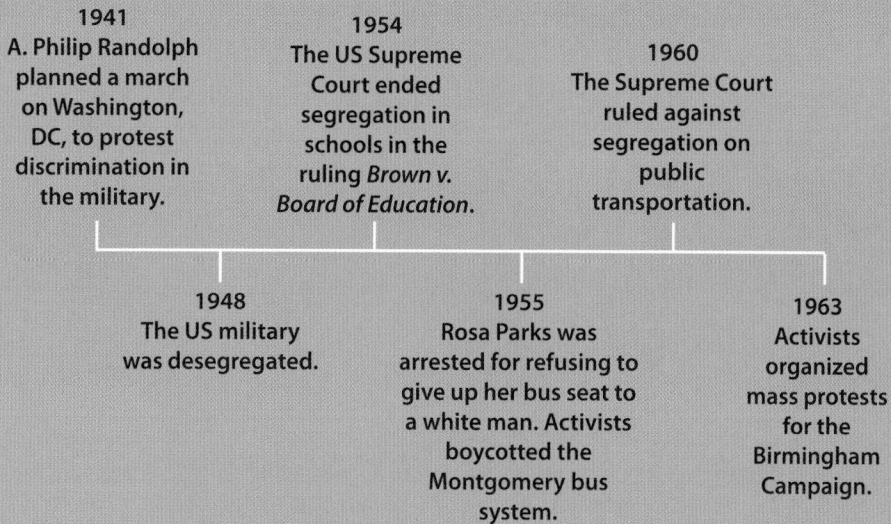

1941
A. Philip Randolph planned a march on Washington, DC, to protest discrimination in the military.

1954
The US Supreme Court ended segregation in schools in the ruling *Brown v. Board of Education*.

1960
The Supreme Court ruled against segregation on public transportation.

1948
The US military was desegregated.

1955
Rosa Parks was arrested for refusing to give up her bus seat to a white man. Activists boycotted the Montgomery bus system.

1963
Activists organized mass protests for the Birmingham Campaign.

The above timeline shows some of the key events leading up to the 1963 March on Washington. How did these events help shape the civil rights movement? How did they lead up to or inspire the march?

were peaceful. But law enforcement officers responded with violence. Police used attack dogs and sprayed protesters with high-pressure fire hoses. Photographers documented these attacks. This media coverage drew more public attention to the civil rights movement. In response to public pressure, the city of Birmingham began to desegregate public places.

PLANNING THE MARCH

After the Birmingham Campaign, activists began planning a new mass protest. Randolph was involved in this planning. He built on his 1941 idea for a march to Washington, DC. Activists called this march the March on Washington for Jobs and Freedom. One of the march's goals was to demand more jobs for African Americans. The unemployment rate among black people was twice as high as it was among white people. Randolph and other organizers understood the importance of increased black employment. It would result in higher incomes. Higher incomes

Activist Bayard Rustin shows the route of the planned March on Washington during a news conference in 1963.

BAYARD RUSTIN

Bayard Rustin had been an adviser to King in the 1950s. Randolph had mentored Rustin. But some activists did not want Rustin to be the main organizer of the March on Washington. Rustin had joined a communist group in the 1930s. Communism was not a popular political view in the United States at the time. Rustin was also openly gay. Gay people were not widely accepted in American society. Some activists did not like Rustin simply for these reasons. Still, many activists admired Rustin's passion for civil rights.

could lift many people out of poverty. The march's organizers also asked for an increase in the minimum wage. Many black people who did find jobs were only paid minimum wage. The earnings they made were barely enough for them to support themselves.

Seven black activists organized the march. Randolph and King were part of this group. The other organizers were Whitney M. Young Jr., James Farmer, Roy Wilkins, and John Lewis. Bayard Rustin was the main organizer of the march. The organizers spread the word about the march.

The march's organizers kept President Kennedy (*third from right*) informed of their plans.

KENNEDY'S ROLE

In June 1963, Randolph and Lewis told President John F. Kennedy about the March on Washington. Kennedy supported the march's goals. But he was also concerned. Civil rights activists often faced violence during protests. People who opposed the protests often showed up to attack the protesters. Kennedy worried this would happen during the march. He feared that trouble during the march could motivate Congress to vote against the Civil Rights Act. Kennedy had proposed this act earlier that month. If it passed into law, it would end segregation in public places.

Despite Kennedy's concerns, the organizers refused to call off the march. They set up an office in New York City. They recruited volunteers. The organizers had planned for approximately 100,000 marchers. But more than twice that many intended to come. They were to arrive from as far away as California. The organizers had to arrange transportation and food for participants. They had to make sure enough doctors and nurses were available to treat people in case of medical emergencies.

The organizers originally planned for a two-day event. They proposed a march around the White House. But Kennedy disliked that idea. So the organizers changed their plans. The march would instead be a one-day event. Participants would march from the Washington Monument to the Lincoln Memorial. That decision convinced Kennedy to go along with the plan.

Buses transported people to and from Washington, DC, for the march.

A PEACEFUL MARCH

Civil rights leaders wanted to open up the march to many people. They thought that inviting a variety of people would help the march receive more national attention. They invited white activists such as Walter Reuther. Reuther was a friend and supporter of King. He had accompanied King on many marches.

The organizers made sure everything ran smoothly. They arranged more than 20 trains and 2,000 buses to help transport people. Hundreds of marchers arrived at the Washington Monument before dawn on the morning of August 28, 1963. The march began there. Shuttle buses escorted people to the monument grounds.

Hundreds of police officers helped direct marchers. Volunteers packed 80,000 box lunches for participants. They also set up water stations along the route.

Among the volunteers were 2,000 marshals. They worked alongside police officers. They kept order during the march. Kennedy had also placed 4,000 military troops on alert. He was prepared to call in 15,000 more to prevent rioting.

Some people expected trouble when the leader of the American Nazi Party threatened to protest the march. The American Nazi Party was a political party that supported Nazi beliefs. It believed that white people were superior to other races. Its leader was George Lincoln Rockwell. Rockwell claimed that 10,000 of his followers would join him to protest the march. But fewer than 90 of his followers showed up. Police officers surrounded them and prevented any violence. Black civil rights leader Malcolm X had threatened violence against Rockwell. Malcolm X attended the march. But he did not encourage violence. All remained calm.

EXPLORE ONLINE

Chapter Three talks about the planning of the March on Washington. The website below gives more facts about the march. How is the information from the website the same as the information in Chapter Three? What new information did you learn from the website?

THE MARCH ON WASHINGTON
abdocorelibrary.com/march-on-washington-and-its-legacy

CIVIL RIGHTS LEADERS

The March on Washington began with singing and speeches near the Washington Monument. Folk singers sang about peace and equality. Among them were Bob Dylan and African American singer Odetta.

The marchers moved from the Washington Monument toward the Lincoln Memorial. Leaders of the march mingled with the marchers. They linked arms as they walked. They sang "We Shall Overcome." This song was the freedom anthem of the civil rights movement.

African American folk singer Odetta performed during the March on Washington.

JOHN LEWIS'S SPEECH

John Lewis gave a speech at the March on Washington. Many of the march's organizers did not like the original draft of Lewis's March on Washington speech. They thought the speech was too negative. Lewis believed that an act such as the Civil Rights Act should have been pushed through Congress years earlier. He criticized the government for the delay in this legislation. Lewis was pressured to tone down his message.

The March on Washington lasted three hours. It was broadcast to many parts of the world. Activists took turns speaking to the crowd. Among the highlights of the event was a speech written by James Farmer. Farmer was one of the organizers of the event and a cofounder of the Congress of Racial Equality (CORE). This civil rights organization had helped organize the Freedom Rides and the March on Washington. Farmer's speech was delivered by CORE member Floyd McKissick. Farmer had been jailed for organizing civil rights protests in

Black performer and activist Josephine Baker gave a speech at the March on Washington.

Louisiana. He wrote that he was with the marchers in spirit.

Although people of many different races and backgrounds came to the march, the speakers were mostly men. Josephine Baker and Daisy Bates were the only two women to speak at the event. Baker was a black entertainer who had found fame in France. In her speech, she talked about the discrimination she had faced in the United States. Bates had helped integrate Little Rock Central High School in Arkansas. She gave a speech that honored the contributions of women to the civil rights movement.

The march's organizers asked the wives of civil rights leaders to march apart from their husbands.

PERSPECTIVES

MIKI CONN

In 1957 Miki Conn and her family moved to Delmar, New York. They were the first black family to live in the area. Conn was inspired by the civil rights movement. She was arrested in 1962 for demonstrating against segregation in Maryland. That experience motivated her to volunteer for the March on Washington. Conn later explained what she learned from the march. She said in an interview: "What the March on Washington showed me is that there are always others who have the same interests . . . and that if you can get them together to think about it and plan about it, you can make changes."

The women were not invited to join a meeting with Kennedy after the march. Women civil rights activists, such as Rosa Parks, were also not invited to the meeting.

Kennedy was thrilled with the success of the event. He was relieved that it had been a peaceful march. Kennedy and the civil rights leaders were hopeful that the march would lead to change.

STRAIGHT TO THE
SOURCE

Josephine Baker was one of the speakers at the March on Washington. In her speech, she encouraged African Americans to speak out against inequality. She said:

Young people must do one thing, and I know you have heard this story a thousand times from your mothers and fathers, like I did from my mama. I didn't take her advice. But I accomplished the same in another fashion. You must get an education. You must go to school, and you must learn to protect yourself. And you must learn to protect yourself with the pen, and not the gun. Then you can answer them, and I can tell you—and I don't want to sound corny—but friends, the pen really is mightier than the sword.

Source: Stephen Papich. *Remembering Josephine.* Indianapolis, IN: Bobbs-Merrill, 1976. Print. 212.

What's the Big Idea?

Take a close look at this passage. What does Baker believe is the best way to fight injustice? Do you agree? Why or why not?

A LIVING LEGACY

Many people were inspired by the March on Washington. But there was still strong opposition to the civil rights movement in the South. On September 15, 1963, a KKK member tunneled under the basement of the Sixteenth Street Baptist Church in Birmingham. He put an explosive device underneath the building. Civil rights leaders such as King regularly used this church for meetings. It was the largest African American church in Birmingham. The bomb went off during Sunday school classes. It killed four black girls and injured 14 people.

The Birmingham bombing in September 1963 sparked mass protests.

Rioting and violence broke out after the bombing. A police officer shot and killed a black teenager. Two white teenagers shot and killed another black teenager. More black people were injured. Alabama's governor brought in hundreds of police officers, National Guardsmen, and state troopers to stop the violence.

A suspect for the bombing was arrested. Despite strong evidence against him,

THE POVERTY RATE

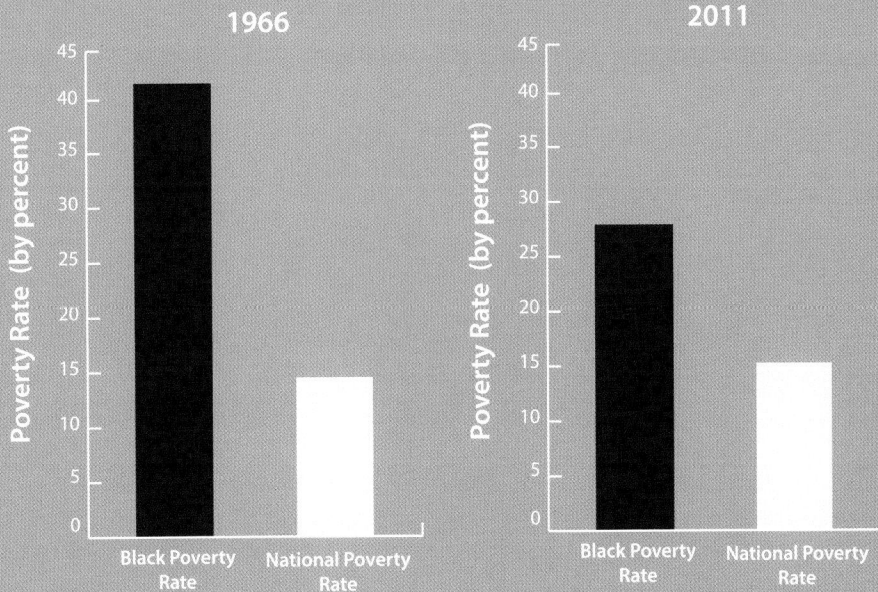

Protests such as the March on Washington led to the creation of better civil rights laws in the 1960s. But black people today are still more likely than white people to live in poverty. The above graph compares the black poverty rate to the national poverty rate in 1966 and 2011. How did the black poverty rate change over this 45-year period?

he was found not guilty. He would only be tried again and found guilty 14 years after the bombing. Two other KKK members were later found guilty of helping to plan the bombing.

Many people around the world were shocked by the Birmingham bombing. Along with other well-publicized events such as the March on Washington, the bombing forced lawmakers to act. The result was the passage of two civil rights acts. The first was the Civil Rights Act of 1964. This act was passed into law by President Lyndon B. Johnson after Kennedy's death. It outlawed segregation in schools and public places. It also made job discrimination illegal. The second act was the Voting Rights Act of 1965. This law made it illegal to prevent African Americans from voting.

GLOBAL INFLUENCE

The March on Washington was broadcast around the world. Thousands of Americans living in Amsterdam, the Netherlands, marched in support of the cause. The mayor of Kingston, Jamaica, also led a march to support the cause.

The spirit of the March on Washington had a lasting effect outside the United States. South African civil rights leader Nelson Mandela was inspired by King.

Leader Nelson Mandela led a movement to end segregation in South Africa in the 1990s.

Mandela worked to end segregation in his country. In South Africa, a system of segregation called apartheid was in place for more than 40 years. White people discriminated against black people. Mandela's efforts helped end apartheid in 1994. Mandela became the country's first black president in that year. In a speech at his election celebration, Mandela quoted part of King's "I Have a Dream" speech.

Much of the march's legacy centers on King. His words and actions on that day helped him win the Nobel Peace Prize in 1964. King was assassinated in 1968. People all over the world mourned his death. In 1983 a national holiday was created in his honor. Martin Luther King Jr. Day is celebrated in January each year.

The March on Washington proved that peaceful protest could inspire change. It brought together people of many backgrounds in support of a common cause. It is remembered today as one of the most iconic protests of the civil rights movement.

INSPIRED BY KING

Many activists today are inspired by King's "I Have a Dream" speech. On the fiftieth anniversary of the March on Washington, activists came together to read the speech aloud. Malala Yousafzai, a Pakistani activist who defends women's educational rights, was among the readers. So were American poet Maya Angelou and Ndileka Mandela, the granddaughter of Nelson Mandela. Their reading of King's speech was broadcast around the world.

STRAIGHT TO THE
SOURCE

On the fiftieth anniversary of the March on Washington, thousands of people gathered near the Lincoln Memorial. President Barack Obama spoke at the event. He said:

> *Because they marched, the civil rights law was passed. Because they marched, the voting rights law was signed. Because they marched, doors of opportunity and education swung open so their daughters and sons could finally imagine a life for themselves beyond washing somebody else's laundry or shining somebody else's shoes. Because they marched, city councils changed and state legislatures changed and Congress changed and, yes, eventually the White House changed. Because they marched, America became more free and more fair.*

> Source: Washington Post Staff. "Full Transcript: President Obama's Speech on the 50th Anniversary of the March on Washington." *Washington Post*. Washington Post, August 28, 2013. Web. Accessed July 31, 2018.

Consider Your Audience

Adapt this passage for a different audience, such as your principal or friends. Write a blog post conveying this same information for the new audience. How does your post differ from the original text and why?

FAST FACTS

- The March on Washington occurred on August 28, 1963. Marchers gathered near the Lincoln Memorial in Washington, DC. They protested discrimination against African Americans and a lack of job opportunities. Approximately 250,000 people attended the march. The marchers were mostly African American, but people of many backgrounds attended the event. It became one of the largest protest gatherings in US history.

- President John F. Kennedy was fearful of violence at the march.

- More than 2,000 buses and 20 trains were arranged to transport marchers.

- Important civil rights activists gave speeches at the march. African American activist Martin Luther King Jr. gave his famous "I Have a Dream" speech at the march.

- The March on Washington led to the enactment of the Civil Rights Act of 1964 and the Voting Rights Act of 1965.

STOP AND
THINK

Tell the Tale

Chapter One of this book describes Martin Luther King Jr.'s "I Have a Dream" speech. Imagine you were at the March on Washington and heard his words. Write 200 words about your experience.

Why Do I Care?

The March on Washington happened more than 50 years ago. But it left a long-lasting legacy. How might your life or your friends' lives be different if the march had not happened?

Surprise Me

Chapter Three discusses the planning of the march. After reading this book, what two or three facts about this topic did you find most surprising? Write a few sentences about each fact. Why did you find each fact surprising?

GLOSSARY

anthem
a song of praise and pride

communist
relating to communism, a political system in which all people in a society share their goods with each other

discrimination
the unjust treatment of a person or group based on race or other perceived differences

integration
the process of bringing together people of different races or backgrounds

marshal
a federal law officer

minimum wage
the lowest wage per hour that an employer is required by law to pay its workers

racism
a belief that a certain race is better than others

riot
violent and uncontrolled behavior in a public place

segregation
the separation of people of different races or ethnic groups through separate schools and other public spaces

ONLINE RESOURCES

To learn more about the March on Washington, visit our free resource websites below.

Core Library CONNECTION
FREE! COMMON CORE MULTIMEDIA RESOURCES

Visit **abdocorelibrary.com** for free Common Core resources for teachers and students, including vetted activities, multimedia, and booklinks, for deeper subject comprehension.

Booklinks NONFICTION NETWORK
FREE! ONLINE NONFICTION RESOURCES

Visit **abdobooklinks.com** for free additional online weblinks for further learning. These links are routinely monitored and updated to provide the most current information available.

LEARN MORE

Watson, Stephanie. *Martin Luther King Jr. and the March on Washington*. Minneapolis, MN: Abdo Publishing, 2016.

Winter, Max. *The Civil Rights Movement*. Minneapolis, MN: Abdo Publishing, 2015.

ABOUT THE AUTHOR

Duchess Harris, JD, PhD

Professor Harris is the chair of the American Studies department at Macalester College and curator of the Duchess Harris Collection of ABDO books. She is the author and coauthor of recently released ABDO books including *Hidden Human Computers: The Black Women of NASA*, *Black Lives Matter*, and *Race and Policing*.

Before working with ABDO, she authored several other books on the topics of race, culture, and American history. She served as an associate editor for *Litigation News*, the American Bar Association Section of Litigation's quarterly flagship publication, and was the first editor in chief of *Law Raza*, an interactive online journal covering race and the law, published at William Mitchell College of Law. She has earned a PhD in American Studies from the University of Minnesota and a JD from William Mitchell College of Law.

INDEX

American Nazi Party, 27

Baker, Josephine, 31, 33
Bates, Daisy, 31
Birmingham bombing, 35–37
Birmingham Campaign, 18–19, 21
Black Codes, 13

Civil Rights Act, 23, 30, 38
Congress of Racial Equality (CORE), 30
Conn, Miki, 32

Evans, Cheryl, 36

Farmer, James, 22, 30–31
Freedom Riders, 17–18, 30

"I Have a Dream" speech, 8, 10, 39, 40

Jackson, Mahalia, 10
Jim Crow laws, 9, 13, 16

Kennedy, John F., 23–24, 26, 32, 38
King, Martin Luther, Jr., 8, 10–11, 18, 22, 25, 26, 35, 40
Ku Klux Klan (KKK), 14, 18, 35, 37

Lee-Payne, Edith, 8
Lewis, John, 18, 22, 23, 30
Lincoln Memorial, 7, 24, 29, 41

Malcolm X, 26, 27
Mandela, Nelson, 38–39, 40
March on Washington Movement, 16
military, US, 15, 16–17, 26

Obama, Barack, 41
Odetta, 29

Parks, Rosa, 17, 32

Randolph, Philip A., 14–16, 21, 22–23
Roosevelt, Franklin D., 15–16
Rustin, Bayard, 22

Supreme Court, US, 17

voting rights, 13–14, 38, 41

Washington Monument, 7, 24, 25–26, 29